You are a Rainbow

Lisa M Buske

ISBN-13:
978-0692235607

ISBN-10:
0692235604

Dedicated to this year's
Kindergarten class...

May you reach your
full potential as you
recognize the Rainbow
you are created to be!

You are...

reliable

rational

remarkable

responsible

rare

radiant

respectful

resourceful

receptive

reasonable

reflective

R

You are...

adaptable

ambitious

appreciative

accepting

articulate

adventurous

authentic

awe-inspiring

affectionate

amiable

athletic

Ra

You are...

intrinsic

inquisitive

important

independent

integral

intelligent

illustrious

i'm peccable

inspirational

influential

inventive

Rai

You are...

noteworthy   natural   novel

neighborly   noble

newsy   nimble

natty

neutral   non-judgmental

Rain   notable

You are...

blessed

business-like

big-thinking

benevolent

believing

bodacious

BOLD

beaming

balanced

brilliant

blissful

R a i n b

You are...

open-minded

original

objective

observant

optimistic

organized

open-handed

obedient

obliging

Outstanding

out going

Rainbo

Wonderful   worthy   Whimsical

You are...

Watchful

wise

Witty

Wealthy

Willing   worldly

Warm-hearted

Well-rounded

Rainbow

Read with me...

I am a

Rainbow!

~ Include picture above ~

Other books by Lisa M Buske

Other Books by Lisa M Buske

<u>Where's Heidi?</u>
<u>One Sister's Journey</u>
Also on Kindle
~One sister's journey following the abduction of her only sister, a journey of hope and learning to trust God again.

<u>When the Waves Subside</u>
<u>There is Hope</u>
Also on Kindle
~A short story to show the strength in the grieving parent

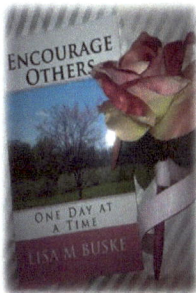

~

<u>Encourage Others</u>
<u>One Day at a Time</u>
An organizational tool to keep track of those important dates

<u>No More Pain: I Can Fly</u>
"No More Pain: I Can Fly" is a short story to remind us there is hope. Death, although sad to those left behind, is only the beginning for our loved ones wearing angel's wings.

http://LisaMBuske.com
http://www.lisambuske.com/blog.html
Email: lbuskewriter@aol.com
Twitter: @LisaBuske
Facebook: "Where's Heidi?"
Mailing: P.O. Box 261, New Haven, New York 13121

Ways to Use This Book

- Read aloud to your child/class to introduce positive characteristics and traits they might not typically learn about

- Read as a bedtime story as a way to trigger conversation about the wonderful and positive attributes you see in your child

- For Older Children/Students:
  - Read aloud to class/youth group and:
    - Have kiddos look up the different words in the dictionary (not online, use a real dictionary)
    - Have kiddos pick one word from each page they feel best describes themselves and then create a Rainbow
      - they could paint, draw, write, or whatever creative way you/they feel best expresses their personal Rainbow acronym
    - Have kiddos write an essay/blog/article using 1 – 2 attributes from each page to encourage them to write creatively
    - Have kiddos create a Rainbow of one of their peers
      - They could draw names anonymously so each person is writing about one other person in the class/group
      - You could do this as a class/group project and have each child create a rainbow for each other – then create a book for each person to keep about themselves – written by their peers
        - NOTE: This would be an extensive project and require time, depending on the number of kiddos in your group/class, one a day/meeting
        - Possibly have a "Celebrate Each Other" day to display and present the project, inviting family/friends or other classes

Be creative and use your Rainbow of gifts to encourage others to do the same, especially our kiddos. I'd love to hear and see some of your ideas ~ feel free to email or share on Facebook.

www.ingramcontent.com/pod-product-compliance
Lightning Source LLC
Chambersburg PA
CBHW040230070426

42448CB00034B/266